I0776386

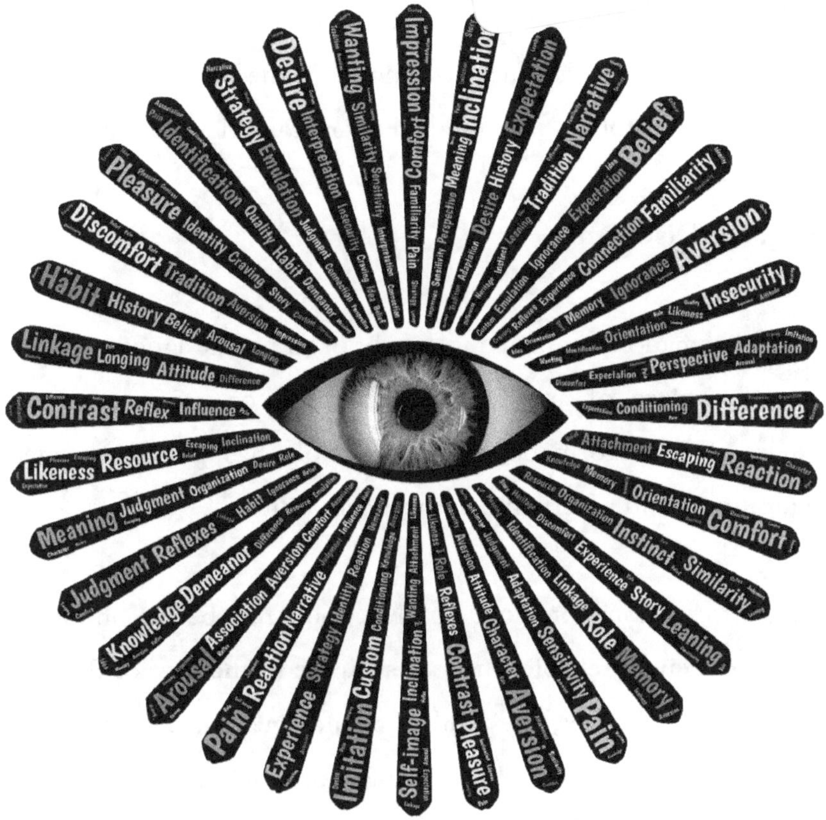

EMOTIONAL INTELLIGENCE

IMPROVE YOUR SOCIAL SKILLS, CONTROL YOUR EMOTIONS & HANDLE DIFFICULT PEOPLE

Text Copyright © Wallace Foulds

All rights reserved. No part of this guide may be reproduced in any form without permission in writing from the publisher except in the case of brief quotations embodied in critical articles or reviews.

Legal & Disclaimer

The information contained in this book is not designed to replace or take the place of any form of medicine or professional medical advice. The information in this book has been provided for educational and entertainment purposes only.

The information contained in this book has been compiled from sources deemed reliable, and it is accurate to the best of the Author's knowledge; however, the Author cannot guarantee its accuracy and validity and cannot be held liable for any errors or omissions. Changes are periodically made to this book. You must consult your doctor or get professional medical advice before using any of the suggested remedies, techniques, or information in this book.

Upon using the information contained in this book, you agree to hold harmless the Author from and against any damages, costs, and expenses, including any legal fees potentially resulting from the application of any of the information provided by this guide. This disclaimer applies to any damages or injury caused by the use and application, whether directly or indirectly, of any advice or information presented, whether for breach of contract, tort, negligence, personal injury, criminal intent, or under any other cause of action.

You agree to accept all risks of using the information presented inside this book. You need to consult a professional medical practitioner in order to ensure you are both able and healthy enough to participate in this program.

CONTENTS

INTRODUCTION

"Any person capable of angering you becomes your master."

Epictetus, Greek philosopher

In 1990, a modern day movement was born through a singular notion called "emotional intelligence", which was coined by psychologists Peter Salovey and John D. Mayer in a paper they co-wrote.

The article describes the potential rewards and hazards when controlling one's emotions in personal and professional settings. The abstract of the article began with the following:

This article presents a framework for emotional intelligence, a set of skills hypothesized to contribute to the accurate appraisal and expression of emotion in oneself and in others, the effective regulation of emotion in self and others, and the use of feelings to motivate, plan, and achieve in one's life.

In the article itself, Salovey, who is currently the President of Yale University, and Mayer, a psychologist at the University of New Hampshire, go deep into the nature of emotional intelligence, writing that they believed that the regulation of emotion, or having "emotional intelligence", might lead one to adapt and reinforce better mood behaviors. Those reinforced mood behaviors could positively enhance an individual's state of mind and the attitude of everyone around them, which could motivate others to mutually rewarding results.

EMOTIONAL INTELLIGENCE

On the other hand, they also believed that sociopaths could expertly use the regulation of their emotions in a negative way to manipulate others to diabolical ends.

The article begins with the rhetorical question, "Is emotional intelligence a contradiction in terms?"

Salovey and Mayer explain the question by citing the views of Western thought that abides by the idea that emotions are a "disorganized interruption of mental activity." The pair of psychologists proceeds to define "emotional intelligence" as a subset of "social intelligence" that involves the ability of a person to monitor their feelings and emotions as well as the feelings and emotions of all the people around them.

Through this process of monitoring their feelings, the person with emotional intelligence can discriminate between them, and use them to guide their behavior, thinking, and ultimate actions in a way that serves them well. The alternative would be to release emotions without any consideration to how they will influence our mood and the mood of the people around us.

People from varying fields of psychology and business define emotional intelligence in numerous ways—some say, in too many ways—as they praise its capacity to take humanity to a higher level. While other people question its relevance, and whether it is good or bad to actively work on one's emotional intelligence in a systematic way.

Regardless of whether emotional intelligence takes people to new heights both personally and professionally, or it is irrelevant to overall human satisfaction, we all must properly analyze its defining characteristics to determine if it has value as one of many tools that we might pull from the toolbox to get us through the world in a more efficient manner.

In this book, we will discuss how you can train yourself to have a higher Emotional Quotient (EQ), learn where you can apply it for maximum benefit, and how to determine whether or not it is being practiced against you for dark purposes by the antisocial members of our society.

EMOTIONAL INTELLIGENCE AND SUCCESS

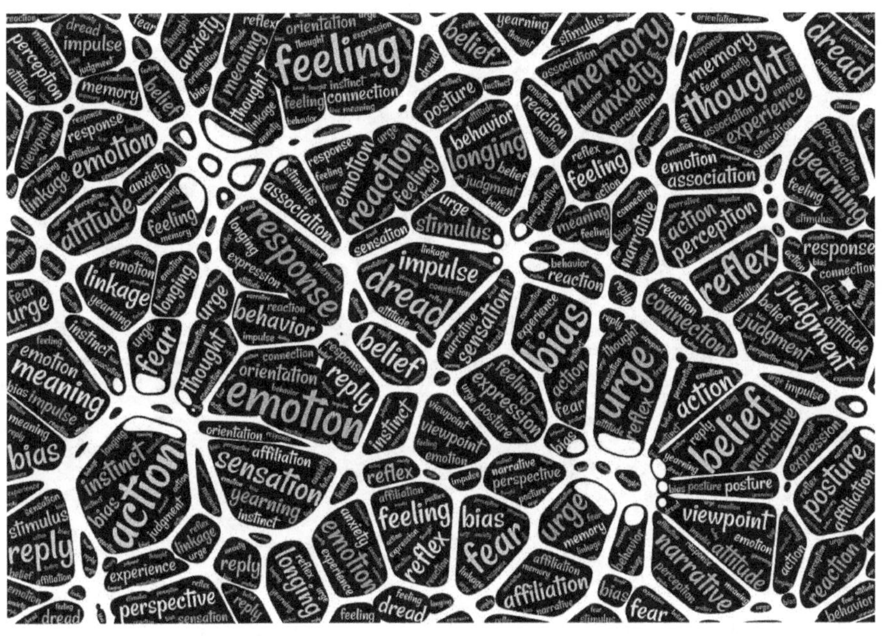

"Life is a series of experiences, each one of which makes us bigger, even though it is hard to realize this. For the world was built to develop character and we must learn that the setbacks and grieves which we endure help us out in marching onward."

Henry Ford, business magnate

People debate EQ endlessly, but a long list of researchers and philosophers have found through studies that EQ is more than a notion; emotional intelligence is a huge factor in determining professional success and personal happiness.

The world's third largest executive search and talent strategy firm, Egon Zehnder International, conducted one of those studies, and after analyzing 515 senior executives, they determined that emotional intelligence was a more important factor to their leadership ability and occupational achievement than IQ or relevant experience.

In fact, across the board, it has been determined that people with average IQs and high EQ outperform those with high IQs around 70 percent of the time.

Research by the Center for Creative Leadership (CCL), a global provider of executive education, found emotional incompetence as the primary reason for executive failure. According to the CCL, ineffective leaders have difficulty adapting to change, do not work well in teams, and develop poor interpersonal relationships.

More proof from the Carnegie Institute of Technology, which later became Carnegie Mellon University, shows that individual financial success is determined though the ability to effectively negotiate, communicate, and lead through a congenial personality. The

EMOTIONAL INTELLIGENCE

institute's study showed that technical ability was important, but not as valuable as skills related to emotional intelligence.

In 1997, Hay/McBer Research and Innovation Group did a study on the success of salespeople within a large national insurance company, and they found that the leading sales generators were self confident, showed initiative, and had empathy. Those emotionally intelligent people benefited greatly, securing policies with an average worth of $114,000 compared to their low EQ counterparts who only averaged $54,000. That is a huge deficit for those who are not emotionally skilled, and a big difference in tax bracket.

Therefore, it is safe to say that the higher a person plans to travel up the organizational ladder, the more important it is to have emotional intelligence because the entire organization feels the decisions when leaders make them from high above.

Although, supervisors at all levels influence the bottom line, and could benefit from emotional intelligence training. A 1999 study conducted by The McClelland Center at a manufacturing plant found decreases in lost-time accidents and less grievances after supervisors trained in emotional competency. The results found by the research division at Hay Group showed that EQ training produced production results that year that exceeded expectations by $250,000.

Clearly, employees are more productive and feel better about themselves and their jobs when their leaders are reliable, rational problem-solvers, trustworthy, empathetic, supportive, and genuinely likable.

Emotionally intelligent people find success because they make great leaders, who excel in employee relationships, and easily adapt to new challenges, shifting environments, and varying personalities. They listen and consider staff feedback, they communicate effectively with their peers and subordinates, and they collaborate to accentuate their strengths and the people they lead, so that no one's weaknesses are on display.

In addition, leaders with emotional intelligence do not look to sabotage anyone or any situation, even when someone on their team is difficult, and that is because they do not hold grudges or even entertain the idea of bitter grievances. In fact, leaders with high EQ have the ability to neutralize toxic people in a healthy way, so that everyone benefits.

They are also valuable because they bring in customers, and they keep the client relationships solid through consideration, empathy, respect, and harmony.

Emotional intelligence is powerful. People with high EQ make an average salary that is $29,000 more a year than the emotionally weak.

EMOTIONAL INTELLIGENCE

They are among every company's top performers. They get more work done with fewer resources. They are healthier in their personal lives, and that health has a positive influence on their work lives. They get more sleep, they have more energy, and they have a wider network of business associates and friends.

If your EQ needs some work, there is plenty of hope. The brain is highly adaptive organ, and as you practice any new skill, your mind builds bridges to it, so that you can get to your destination easier in the future. In time, the new path becomes so clear that healthy habits form.

Keep reading to find out how to train your brain to reach for rational solutions, instead of highly charged emotional decisions, which are hardly decisions at all.

On the other hand, you cannot learn to have a higher "IQ" because your intelligence quotient has nothing to do with the *amount* of knowledge you gain as you mature, but rather how you quickly you adapt and learn, and that is hardwired into your brain. Therefore, you are stuck with your IQ, but your EQ can grow stronger through diligent effort and ambitious training.

ARE YOU ALREADY EMOTIONAL INTELLIGENT?

"Anyone can be angry—that is easy. But to be angry with the right person, to the right degree, at the right time, for the right purpose, and in the right way—that is not easy."

Aristotle, Greek philosopher and scientist

In 85 BCE, a boy was born in Syria with very little hope that he would become anything in his life.

The Syrian was either born a slave or became a slave when the Roman Empire reduced Syria to a province under General Pompey the Great.

At the age of 12, the boy was brought to Rome and given the name Syrus because it was custom for slaves to take the name of the province from where they were born.

Scholars say that Syrus was a remarkable boy who won people over through his intelligence, wit, and physically "fair" qualities that were far superior to his age and the conditions of his upbringing as a slave in an overrun province.

Enamored with the beauty of his person and the elegance of his manners, Syrus's master provided the growing boy with a proper, liberal education, and then offered his freedom to him. When the young man became a free person, he took the name Pubililus, which scholars believe is the surname of his former master.

In his late teens, "Pubililus Syrus" was born.

Pubililus became an actor in mimes, which the people of the times considered great theater. He even performed before Julius Caesar, and then became a mime writer. Because of his outstanding talent and great personality, he grew famous for his improvisational skills, before becoming somewhat of a philosophical poet.

Today, all that is left of his total works are 700 writings, which he produced in iambic and trochaic verse, and deal mostly with morality.

You might have already figured out that Pubililus was emotionally intelligent, and able to control his emotions in order to make his way from a slave, with very little possibility of a future worth remembering, to a name that we remember today, and a person that university students study.

Pubililus believed that fear holds people back, and valor comes to us by being daring. He said that a good reputation is more important than money, and that debt is the bondage of the free man.

He also believed that wrongdoing for a good cause was virtuous, that avarice is the lacking of all things, that it is foolish to be straightforward with a shameless person, and that "anyone can hold the helm when the sea is calm."

Moreover, while the term "emotional intelligence" might have found its way into the human psyche in 1990, the idea that it is beneficial to control one's mood, temper, and tone has surfaced from his philosophical musings that are more than 2,000 years old.

Pubililus stated in the first century BCE something that we still pass along today as pure truth: "Rule your feelings, lest your feelings rule you."

I wonder, was Syrus born with emotional intelligence, or did he learn it because of his high degree of intellectuality? What comes first?

There are questions that you can ask yourself in order to determine if you are already emotionally intelligent, as provided by Daniel Goleman, the writer of *Emotional Intelligence*, and the person who began the modern emotional intelligence movement in 1995, which we will discuss in detail later in the book.

If you answer "YES" to all of the following questions, you certainly have the capacity for high emotional intelligence, but this is just a "taste", not a test.

1) Are you aware of your feelings, and the cause of them?

2) Are you aware of your limitations and strengths as a leader?

3) Do you manage your emotions well and recover quickly when something upsets you?

4) Do you have the ability to adapt to changing circumstances?

5) Do you stay focused on your goals, and know the steps to fulfill them?

6) Are you aware of the feelings of the people in which you interact, and understand their way of viewing things?

7) Do you have the ability to persuade and use your influence effectively?

8) Can you settle conflicts in a satisfactory way through negotiation?

9) Do you work well on a team?

Did you find your answer from these questions? Are you halfway to being a person with a high EQ? Let us go a step further to see if you have the intangibles that make up an emotionally intelligent person.

Essentially, high EQ is an abstract quality with varying defining characteristics that depend on the expert psychologist doing the analysis, but the following behaviors provide the basic nature of a person with high EQ, and if one struggles in any one of these areas, refinement is required in order to become more emotionally intelligent human being.

General Happiness

We should start with the most important trait, which extends beyond office complexes and board meetings to our everyday existence. **If you are seeking to become emotionally intelligent, do not allow anyone but YOU to dictate YOUR pursuit of HAPPINESS.**

An emotionally intelligent person does not allow anyone to take away his or her good feelings when they accomplish something that required hard work and brought joy. The opinions of other people should not be completely ignored because constructive criticism can be beneficial when applied to future endeavors, but moments of happiness should not be dissolved by the remarks of others, especially if they are rude in nature.

Insecure people who are not on your level will try to sabotage your happiness by attempting to take away your shining moments. Your self-worth comes from within, and not from the critics who attempt to find a backdoor to your insides in order to create chaos within you.

Negativity

Negative thoughts enter and exit the minds of emotionally intelligent people very quickly. We have no control over the many ways that negativity enters our thoughts, but people with a high EQ do not allow those ideas to ruminate for hours, or days, or more. An emotionally intelligent person considers the negative thoughts, and then, the person explores the rational facts behind the situation, as they quickly adjust their feelings to incorporate the truth of the matter.

Our human bodies are equipped with threat mechanisms that put us on guard, and those mechanisms place our sensitivities and senses on high alert. Some people feel the impact of this mechanism more than other individuals feel it, because of past traumatic events that have created an emotional or mental behavior disorder.

However, a person with emotional intelligence does not allow irrational ideas to infect his or her thinking for long lengths of time. After he or she evaluates the emotions, a new and positive outlook forms, which the person bases on rational information. Thereby, "the rational" replaces "the irrational negativity".

Grudges

Emotionally intelligent people do not hold on to grudges. They move towards a new direction because grudges create stress and hold people back from going forward. Grudges are another survival response that keeps humans from becoming complacent around a person who might hurt us in some form or fashion.

However, the best defense to neutralize a person's ability to infect you with negativity is to let go of "them", the events around "them", and the stress that accompanies "them". Anxiety about the situation or revenge against the person is not the route of an emotionally intelligent individual. Grudges do not assist with emotional or mental health, and they are a distraction from productivity and focus on things that involve the present and future, not the past.

Thick Skin

It is very difficult to offend a person with emotional intelligence. In fact, they tend to be light-hearted in regards to their faults and imperfections. They have a sense of humor about themselves, and might even be self-deprecating without being self-loathing.

This does not mean that they allow others to degrade them, but they are self-confident and have an open mind; therefore, they have a thick skin and cannot be shaken whenever they are faced with something that might be construed by others as a personal insult.

Perfection

Emotionally Intelligent people do not expect perfection out of themselves in every situation. The human quality that is certain, and defines us more than any other, is our fallibility. Human beings fall all the time. We fail ourselves and the people in our lives on a regular basis. Although, is it really "failure" or a bridge to future success?

Failure can be turned into resiliency, and resiliency along with hard work and practice, makes us better. In other words, emotionally intelligent people never strive for perfection because it is IMPOSSIBLE, and people with high EQ understand this.

If you are a perfectionist, you do not have a high EQ because it takes an extraordinary amount of time for a perfectionist to get anything done, while the person with emotional intelligence produces solid work as they do laps around. They know perfection is not a possibility because everyone has a different view of what "perfect" means.

Therefore, the perfectionist is always failing, and that is not good on anyone's self-esteem, and a low self-esteem leads to reduced production and effort. Feel good about the things you have achieved, and find excitement in the next task ahead, instead of the task that was a tad less than perfect and something you believe should have done in a different manner. Move on if you are looking to improve your emotional intelligence.

Mistakes

Emotionally intelligent peopled do not forget their mistakes when turning to new tasks, but they do not dwell on them either. They do not repeat the same mistakes because they want to improve themselves on a daily basis, but they do not allow themselves to become anxious when given the chance to do better the next time that a similar situation faces them.

Emotional Self-Awareness

People with emotional intelligence can identify their emotions, and from where they stemmed. People who are unable to understand their emotions make irrational choices and are not productive in tending to their emotions in an impactful way.

Those people who are able to label their emotions might find it hard to believe that 64 percent of the population does not have the ability to describe their negative emotions beyond simple adjectives like mad, sad, and bad.

Emotionally intelligent people break down their emotions further to descriptors like irritable, anxious, frustrated, and ashamed; therefore, they have the ability to compartmentalize them, and find rational ways to dissolve them and move forward.

Strengths and Weaknesses

Understanding emotions is only one piece of the many traits that make up an emotionally intelligent people. **Understanding strengths and weaknesses is another crucial component of high EQ**. They understand the types of people and the particular environments that produce their best results and push them to higher successes. On the other hand, in order to keep their weaknesses from holding them from moving upward, they are honest about them, and work to fix them.

While they work on their weaknesses, emotionally intelligent people delegate tasks to individuals that are more qualified in their weak areas, or work with others in teams to create a symbiotic relationship in which everyone brings their strengths to the table and all members succeed in their endeavors.

Giving and Receiving

Emotionally intelligent people give *without* the expectation that they will receive something in return. Although healthy relationships are not one-sided, there should never be conditions that go along with acts of kindness. Whether it is time, advice, or a material gift, a person with a high EQ never considers what they will receive in return. Instead, they are genuinely thoughtful, and build strong relationships through their intuition of others' need, and what makes people happy.

Toxic People

Toxic people exist to make our lives hell, but **an emotionally intelligent person does not allow difficult people to frustrate or exhaust them**. On top of that, they neutralize these sorts of people by allowing them to have a point of view, and even consider their standpoint in order to find common ground, so that chaos does not derail any situation that is in front of them. A rational approach in a time of conflict is effective against irrational people in most cases.

Curiosity

Regardless of their personality type, whether an extrovert or introvert, individuals with a high EQ are genuinely interested in the people around them, and those people notice. Curiosity is inside those who have empathy, and their care and concern for people opens up the world to all possibilities, as people open up to them.

Appreciation

People who have emotional intelligence are grateful for the things in their life. They do not dwell on the things they do not have, but cultivate gratitude for the things they do have, and because of it, they are less anxious and have more energy.

Change

Emotionally intelligent people adapt to new environments quickly. They do not wait around in fear, hoping for something different to appear, or for the status quo to reappear. When change comes into focus, people with a high EQ usually already have a plan in place to incorporate the new outcomes into their lives, so they never miss a step.

Character Judgment

Social awareness is a character trait of the emotionally intelligent, and with that trait comes the ability to read other people and determine their motivations and whether or not they have integrity. In other words, **people with high EQ are a good judge of character**.

Self-Control

Many people have difficult saying "no" to other people, and they also have a hard time maintaining control over their own impulses. People who say "yes" to everything burnout quickly, experience stress, and suffer from depression. **Emotionally intelligent people do not overfill their plate by offering to do everything that people ask** of them, and they only take on new task if there is time available to do them. Saying "no" shows self-control and the ability to avoid impulsive actions by delaying gratification.

Disconnection

People with sound emotional intelligence are not workaholics, and are very happy to disconnect from their job and the world for a moment. Emotionally intelligent people give themselves time away from the communication grid and live in the moment on a regular basis. Doing this lowers their stress levels, and increases their production when they are at work.

Sleep and Caffeine

Emotionally intelligent people get plenty of rest, and do not count on caffeine to provide them with energy. Sleep recharges the body and mind, and is crucial to reducing stress, increasing production, and keeping a sound and emotionally intelligent mind functioning in the most optimal fashion. Sleep increases memory, attention, and assists with self-control during the course of busy and unpredictable days.

Relying on caffeine to provide you with all of these things is detrimental. Caffeine increases irrational thinking because it induces rapid responses instead of well thought-out responses during the mad rush of each day.

TEACH YOURSELF EMOTIONAL INTELLIGENCE

- -

"Education is the ability to listen to almost anything without losing
your temper or your self-confidence."

- -

Robert Frost, Poet

In 1936, while studying motivation and attitude as it applies to emotion, psychologist Paul Thomas Young described pure emotion as a "complete loss of cerebral control" without a "trace of conscious purpose."

Young defined emotions further in 1943, while the world was at war, as "acute disturbances of the individual as a whole."

Around the same time, psychologists Laurence F. Shaffer, B. Von Holler Gilmer, and Max Schoen wrote that emotion was "a disorganized response, largely visceral, resulting from the lack an effective adjustment."

As you can see, "emotions" have gotten a bad rap for quite some time, especially, the unadulterated kinds of hot feelings.

There is a second school of thought regarding emotion, though. In 1948, Dr. Robert Leeper characterized emotion as a motivating force that helps humans "arouse, sustain, and direct activity;" therefore, emotions are not chaotic and a show of immaturity. Leeper believed that physiological and behavioral changes that occur within the human body, as emotions form, help people prepare for necessary responses in the moment.

In much the same way that we feel heat when we touch a hot stove in order to avoid further injury, emotions keep us in check, so that we do not walk precariously into bad situations. In addition, we can enjoy the good events that occur during the course of the day because positive feelings guide us there.

In all purposes, emotion is a response system that coordinates physiological and cognitive changes in our personal atmosphere into an understandable experience of moods and feelings.

The other end our discussion about emotional intelligence is the "intelligence" part, which society simply defines as "the aggregate or global capacity of an individual to act purposefully, to think rationally, and to deal effectively with his environment."

Given that definition, and what we know about emotion, work is required to align the two, and that is why "emotional intelligence" has become a phenomenon. It is such a simple idea, but so hard for most people to practice and put it into operation.

We know that emotion serves a purpose and keeps us out of harm's way by alerting us of possible dangerous situations and characters, but we must tame our survival instinct to mesh with a modern world. In other words, we must evolve our emotions to match our current stage of evolution. At one point in human history, our emotional instinct built our intelligence, and now that we are highly intelligent, we must use intelligence and rationality to build stable emotions.

Today, the psychology of emotion has grown into a cottage industry, and there is so much to absorb and figure out. Finding truth in the matter is difficult because there is an industry that supports the notion of emotional intelligence, from consulting, education, training, testing, and publishing. As we all know, when anyone invests "money" into an idea to make "more money", objectivity loses its way, making truth harder to find.

We are here to find the truth about EQ.

Your Rational Brain

EQ consists of four elements that deal with both personal emotions and emotions as they apply interpersonally in social situations.

The four elements all work together in harmony to create emotional intelligence. In other words, you must SELF-MANAGE your SELF-AWARENESS in an appropriately rational manner. Self-management and self-awareness are the first two elements. The second set of skills involves your ability to MANAGE RELATIONSHIPS through SOCIAL AWARENESS.

Thereby, these four areas involve what you can sense, and what you do with those things that you sense, on a personal and social level.

EMOTIONAL INTELLIGENCE

As we have discussed, self-awareness is the ability to be aware and understand our emotions, as well as understand the genesis of those emotions. Self-managing them requires the use of the awareness in a flexible manner in order to direct them in a positive way. Rigid emotions create irrational chaos and negative results, which lead to all manner of personally unhealthy consequences.

Social awareness is the ability to be aware of the moods and motives of other people, and social management requires effective responses to those behaviors in order to build and improve partnerships as they grow, to create healthy, symbiotic relationships.

These things are very different from you IQ, which measures intellect, and there is no connection between EQ and IQ, according to research. In other words, you cannot evaluate your EQ by simply knowing your IQ. There is no correlation.

Furthermore, IQ is not flexible. It is static. EQ can move. Traumatic events in our lives can shape our emotional intelligence in a negative way, and the opposite is true as well. If we are mentally and physically healthy because of positive events, our emotional health improves.

Some individuals are instinctively healthy in all phases of their life, and do not allow negative events or people to intrude upon their emotional health. However, sometimes fate decides your physical and mental health because of genetics, or because you experienced trauma as a child or as a soldier or first-responder who now suffers from PTSD. In these cases, you must learn to become emotional healthy in order to become emotionally intelligent.

The bottom line essence of emotional intelligence is focusing your attention in one direction, and that direction is general happiness, which carries all other goals along with it. To find general happiness, you must learn and practice the traits that define emotional intelligence, and science tells us that we can improve our EQ. Emotional intelligence involves the effective communication between the emotional side of your brain and the rational side of your brain.

Your senses enter the brain through the limbic system, and emotions generate here before they ever enter the part of our brain that produces rational thinking. Our first instinct is to react to the sensation in an emotional way because the sensation and all of the emotion that comes with it has not entered our intellect yet. This occurs in this order to protect us from dangers in our environment, and is most commonly referred to as a human's flight-or-fight response.

The light-or-fight response is a purely physiological reaction to a PERCEIVED threat that instinctively makes humans want to fight to protect themselves or run from the hazard that is front of them. However, that perception is not always the reality, and people with a high EQ understand when they are in real danger and when their body PERCEIVES real danger. If you want to improve your emotional intelligence, you must learn the difference.

Neurologists use the word plasticity to describe the mind's adaptive nature. Adaptation comes from experience and practice. Although our IQ remains the same, and IQ predicts our ability to adapt and learn, practice of anything reshapes our ability to do things better. The amount of practice needed to learn a new skill depends on IQ. Some individuals will require more emotional intelligence training than other people, but anyone with enough persistence can learn a new skill because of the brain's plasticity.

Billions of neurons line the path from the limbic system to the brain's rational centers. With each new day of emotional practice, cells connect and rewire in partnerships that create growth. This allows practiced behavior to become predictable behavior. The habits that form through predictable behavior can be both good and bad, depending on what you practice.

In the case of emotional intelligence, practicing good emotional habits will lead to a higher EQ, and destructive responses will fade to gray and then go missing over the course of time.

Practicing Emotional Intelligence

In order to gain a high EQ, you must turn to the experts in the field. It takes a while to read, research, and gather information into distinct ways to practice emotional intelligence, so we did it for you.

First, you want to practice those skills that top firms look for in hiring employees, and promoting those employees into leadership positions. The World Economic Forum released a Future of Jobs Report that detailed the essential skills that workers will need to be successful in 2020.

The top 10 characteristics found by the Swiss nonprofit business-shaping foundation are the following:

1) Complex problem solving
2) Critical thinking
3) Creativity
4) People management
5) Coordination with others
6) Emotional intelligence
7) Judgment and decision-making
8) Service orientation
9) Negotiation
10) Cognitive flexibility

EMOTIONAL INTELLIGENCE

Interestingly, emotional intelligence ranks 6th, but the irony is that nearly all of the other skills require emotional intelligence. Creativity and cognitive flexibility, which is essentially IQ, are the only two traits that do not positively align with EQ.

A survey done by online employment website CareerBuilder in 2011 revealed that the 71 percent of hiring managers preferred a high EQ to a high IQ. In addition, 75 percent of those same managers said they would be more likely to promote a person with emotional intelligence. Furthermore, 59 percent said they would not even higher a person if they had a low EQ.

Therefore, emotional intelligence practice is essential if you want to be successful in the business world.

Six Seconds CEO Joshua Freedman asked a worldwide network of emotionally intelligence practitioners to recommend ways that people could practice to improve their EQ.

Six Seconds is a community of people devoted to the study, research, practice, and execution of emotional intelligence in order to better the world. Freedman broke down the expert responses into a three-step process of practice:

- Increase self-awareness
- Evaluate emotions in a rational way

- Move forward purposefully

Practicing Your Self Awareness

When practicing self-awareness, you are looking to enhance your emotional vocabulary, as discussed already, and increase your awareness and understanding of your feelings. In addition, you need to be able to label those feelings, as well as look for patterns and identify recurring reactions to emotions. The following is some guidance for practice provided by purveyors of the craft of EQ and offered to us by Six Seconds.

"Acknowledge emotions, not as good or bad, right or wrong, but as a source of information that help you gain self-awareness."

Tang Weng Liang

Often, we get hung up in an antagonistic relationship with our emotions. We attempt to suppress them because we consider them bad news. Emotional intelligence has nothing to do with suppressing feelings. EQ has everything to do with treating emotions like data, which our brains provide to us for assistance. Therefore, the first step to self-awareness is taking the valuable information found inside the emotional data, so that we can create something dynamic and useful from it.

EMOTIONAL INTELLIGENCE

Whenever you feel an emotion from now on, label it for its true nature, but not with simple adjectives like "good" or "bad", and then associate it as data. You will find liberation in treating it as information and not your enemy.

"When I find myself reacting to a situation, I take a moment and name the emotion."

Nicole Tervalon

We established that the first thing we should do when an emotion strikes us is to accept it as data, and not our enemy. We also said that it is a good practice to identify the feelings for their true nature.

Malcolm, who is a character that is based on Malcolm III of Scotland in Shakespeare's *Macbeth*, said to "give sorrow words", and it is a great thing to practice. Describing your emotions when you are feeling anxious provides courage and reduces stress and fear. Avoiding emotions and attempting to shrug them off or disable them in some way does nothing to improve the situation at hand.

Psychologists at UCLA proved this notion by exposing 88 people with arachnophobia to tarantula spiders. The psychologists broke up the research participants into four groups. The researchers told the first group to describe their emotions and to label their reactions to the large spider. One example description that the researchers gave for this group was the following response: "I'm anxious and frightened by the ugly, terrifying spider."

The second group used terms that did not convey their feelings of fear, but attempted to use mind-over-matter. For example, research participants in this group might say, "That little spider can't hurt me; I'm not afraid of it."

The third group was told to say something that was irrelevant to the topic of interest, that being THE SPIDER, in an attempt to block out their anxious feelings by avoiding the subject matter entirely.

The last group said nothing, which must have been frustrating for those spider-fearing folks.

Next, the researchers asked their subjects to get as close to the spider as possible, and to touch it if they found the courage to do so. In the end, the psychologists found that the first group, who described their emotions and fear and did not avoid their honest feelings about the spider, got much closer to the tarantula and showed less physiological distress, like sweaty palms, than the subjects in the other three groups.

"The implication," said Michelle Craske, a professor of psychology at UCLA and the senior author of the study, "is to encourage patients, as they do their exposure to whatever they are fearful of, to label the emotional responses they are experiencing and label the characteristics of the stimuli—to verbalize their feelings. That lets people experience the very things they are afraid of, and say, 'I feel scared and I'm here.' They're not trying to push it away and say it's not so bad. Be in the moment and allow yourself to experience whatever you're experiencing."

Other Research has shown this method to be incredibly effective at reducing the intensity of an emotion.

"Notice when you set yourself up for low EQ moments that become low EQ habits."

Marek Helstrom

Marek went on to say that there are two common traps. The first trap is passing critical judgment on others, for example the might say, "How stupid is that?" or "What in the world were they thinking?"

These kinds of comments are a crutch to elevate or affirm one's superiority over another person. The emotionally intelligent moment begins when you learn to recognize the habit and then re-train yourself to restrain from making *any* negative comment at all.

The second trap is taking offense unnecessarily. Many people struggle with this trap. It is hard! Today's society teaches us to take offense at the most trivial situations. By taking offense, and feeling offended, people quickly escalate to criticism, judgment, and bitterness, which all hurt relationships and our own health and well-being.

In these situations, simply notice the other person's comment or action, and instead of taking offense and then taking it personally, just consider it as data, just as we would consider our own emotions as data. We can take interest in the emotion and its possible cause, we can ponder what might be troubling the person who said the hurtful things, or we can assume it is stress related, but taking it to heart, as a personal offense, does not show emotional intelligence. This one requires a lot of patience and a lot of practice.

Here are some other ideas for practicing the self-awareness aspect of emotional intelligence from other people who are practitioners themselves:

- Shabbir Latif: "Train yourself to sense your emotions via sensations in your body."

- Dawn Karner: "Be an observer of yourself. Pay attention to what you feel, and how those feelings contribute, distract, enhance, or challenge you."

- Carolyn Meacher: "Notice your own strengths, and live into your strengths more fully."

- Irina Sergeeva: "Acknowledge your emotions, where you feel them in your body, and name them. Give yourself one minute for this when you feel uneasy. Then, a second step is to ask yourself: 'What can I do about it?' Allow one minute to come up with a solution."

- Avtar Saksena: "Sit silently for 15 minutes every day and do self-introspection. The reflection is a first step towards practicing EQ."

- Cheryl McKenzie-Cook: "Start by noticing what you're feeling right now. Observe without judgment or trying to 'fix' anything; just notice your emotions a few times per day."

Practice Evaluation and Moving Forward Purposefully

In order to practice the second and third parts of emotional intelligence, which includes evaluating emotions in a rational way and moving forward with a purpose, you must apply consequential thinking. This requires you to pause and evaluate the pragmatic and emotional components of every situation, and then navigate the emotions by engaging them and pushing the situation forward.

Afterwards, engage the underlying motivations of the situation in order to strengthen the inner drive to proceed in a useful way.

Finally, exercise optimism in order to identify all opportunities and possibilities that could benefit from the initial emotion.

Sounds a little convoluted, I suppose, so let us take it a step at a time by looking at the advice of other people who practice emotional intelligence and have seen results from it.

"Pause. Acknowledge your thoughts and feelings. Clear your mind."

Nehad Tadros

This three-step process gives you power. The *pause* provides a chance to get back to your baseline emotional state. According to Six Seconds, it takes about "six seconds" for the body to absorb emotion after the emotion has been released– hence, the name of the organization.

Next, *acknowledge* the emotions, which allow your cognitive function and rational thought to slide in there to assist you. After the pause and acknowledgement, your brain will begin to *clear*.

"Ask yourself: "Do I feel expanded and open or contracted and small?"

Rita Haque

EMOTIONAL INTELLIGENCE

When you feel "compressed," breathing deeply right into your belly releases the muscles from the heat they are feeling from that hot emotion. It is important to REALLY BREATH, and to also open your shoulders and relax.

As your lungs fill up, that physiological expansion of the body impacts the state of your mind and your emotions, too, to reduce stress and increase your openness. These things help us make powerful and positive changes in our emotions, and allow us to put those newly arranged feelings to good use for healthier outcomes.

"In challenging situations, I examine my thoughts with the three questions of optimism:

➢ **Am I thinking that this is permanent? ('It will never get better')**

➢ **Am I feeling this is pervasive? ('It is changing everything')**

➢ **Am I giving up my power? ('There is nothing I can do')"**

Sandeep Kelkar

Kelkar continues: "Then I step back and become a 'detective', and try to gather evidence for those views. If those thoughts are inaccurate, I dispute them and choose realistic, accurate, positive thoughts."

Here are some other ideas for practicing the evaluation and forward-moving aspect of emotional intelligence from other practitioners.

- Dawn Cook: "When you hit a setback, separate what parts of the situation you can control or influence and what parts you cannot. Focus on what you can influence and notice how much more confident you feel about overcoming the setback."

- Niloufer Aga: "When you are frustrated or upset, before you say something harsh, take a six second pause to quickly assess the costs and benefits of that action. When you apply consequential thinking, you make more careful choices that ultimately work to your advantage."

- Joshua Freedman: "Find something impossible to do… and practice. It sounds corny but it's a profound mental switch. Just try saying, "I can't" and "I can't yet"—the emotional experience is dramatically different. The first is a wall. The second, a door."

- Beth Hammett: "Take Two: Set aside two minutes—relax and breathe deeply. Then write down two solutions to your problem."

- Dexter Valles: "Create opportunities to informally share what you feel and ask for feelings feedback—in your teams as well as with clients. This can clear the air of any harbored darkness in the relationship."

- Carolyn Meacher: "Tap into compassion everywhere. Engage in positive caring dialogue with the taxi driver, the dry cleaning man, the grocery bag packer, etc. Say good morning to passing people on the sidewalk. Ask meaningful questions. Really listen to the answers."

- Teresa Veenstra: "Take the six second pause to gather your thoughts before you speak."

- Ed Wood: "Learn from the past, live in the moment, and plan for the future."

- Mala Kapadia: "When you are emotionally charged, take a deep breath before responding. The science of breathing is very deep in Yoga, and at least one deep breath creates a Six Second Pause."

UNLOCK YOUR EMOTIONAL GENIUS

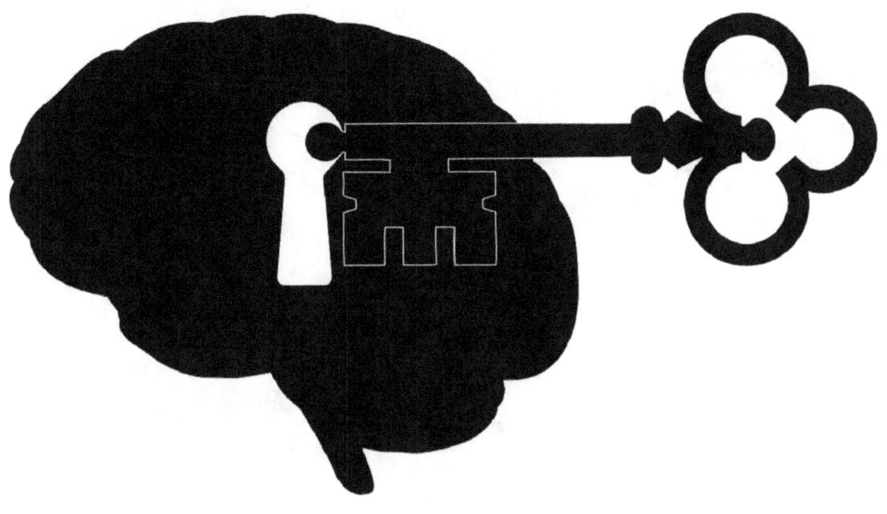

- -

"I know that I am intelligent because I know that I know nothing."

- -

Socrates

Greek Philosopher Pythagoras of Samos, who lived from 570-495 BCE, and came up with everyone's favorite math theorem, thought it was best to divide mood and intelligence from one another, in order to form reason, saying that "intelligence and passion are possessed by other animals, but reason by man alone."

Many years later, 1995 to be exact, emotional intelligence became the talk of psychologists and ambitious people looking to get ahead of their peers because of a book that hit bestseller lists. The book titled *Emotional Intelligence* was on the *New York Times* bestseller list for 18 months.

Daniel Goleman is the author of the book and many other books on social and emotional learning, ecology, meditation, and transparency. He studied at Harvard and in India, where he spent time with Neem Karoli Baba, a Hindu guru and mystic.

Recently, Goleman got into a debate with University of Pennsylvania professor Adam Grant about the importance of EQ.

Grant believes that cognitive ability trumps any talk of emotional intelligence, declaring it as overrated, and saying, "I believe it is a mistake to base hiring or promotion decisions on EQ."

He produced studies to back his beliefs, and offered this caveat in an article on Linkedin:

"This isn't to say that emotional intelligence is useless. It's relevant to performance in jobs where you have to deal with emotions every day, like sales, real estate, and counseling. If you're selling a house or helping people cope with tragedies, it's very useful to know what they're feeling and respond appropriately. But in jobs that lack these emotional demands—like engineering, accounting, or science—emotional intelligence predicted lower performance. If your work is primarily about dealing with data, things, and ideas rather than people and feelings, it's not necessarily advantageous to be skilled in reading and regulating emotions. If your job is to fix a car or balance numbers in a spreadsheet, paying attention to emotions might distract you from working efficiently and effectively."

Goleman, commonly referred to as the grandfather of EQ, called Grant's words an "acerbic take-down of emotional intelligence." He also said that he does not take his arguments very seriously, saying "Academics are fastidious about their research and methods, and analyze their data to see, for example, what variables correlate at what strength."

In other words, there are two realities at play: what works in a laboratory and what works in the real world of the workplace. Goleman's argument is that IQ helps people build the credentials to get the job, but EQ helps the person advance from that starting position because their overall performance in the office is better than the people around them, who are competing for the same leadership positions, but have low emotional intelligence.

"Still, if a computer can model everything you do in your job, emotional intelligence probably will not make or break your daily effectiveness," Goleman says. "But even if you are a solo bench engineer coming up with a better widget, no one will pay attention to you unless you can communicate, persuade, and excite people about that widget—and that takes emotional intelligence."

If you work alone, and do not need to empathize with anyone, or need to cooperate or influence, a high IQ is sufficient for success. Who works in this sort of bubble, though? Not very many people.

Clearly, you need to become an emotional genius to move up the chain of command at your office. Since you will not find EQ knowledge in your university textbooks and professors of core subjects do not teach it you, you must learn it on your own if you were not born with it.

Therefore, until EQ becomes second nature to you, you must practice it, and we have put together the ultimate list of things to practice, so that you can eventually dominate the workplace, or your home, through smart emotional choices

The Keys to Unlocking Your Emotional Intelligence

Breathe like you mean it. We breathe, but do not take much time to appreciate it. In the middle of a storm, take a minute to breathe instead of heading into the eye of it. Stress hits even those people with a super high EQ. The response is the key to emotional intelligence, and while you are practicing solid EQ, you might need to step away from the moment to gather yourself and BREATHE before you can make a rational decision on how to proceed.

Practice observing and connecting to your emotions in the heat of a hectic day. Set a timer that goes off every four or five hours. When the timer goes off, take a few deep breaths, and take account of how you are feeling. Consider how you feel physically and mentally along with the condition of your emotions. Consider why those emotions are present, and if they contribute to an unhealthy feeling, consider the source of the emotion, and begin to formulate a way to fix right the ship.

Pay attention to your behavior when you practice your emotional awareness. Name your emotions and notice how each particular emotion contributes to your current behavior. In addition, consider how each emotion plays out over the course of the day as you consciously attempt to correct the emotion and the affect it has on you in your day-to-day life.

Take responsibility for your feelings and do not blame others for them. Your emotions are your responsibility and no one else's. No one can make you "feel" a certain way. You need to be in control of your emotions by claiming ownership of them, which includes not allowing anyone to own them for even a second. Accept responsibility for how you feel and behave even when you are in the presence of a toxic person who appears like a magician with the ability to transform the emotions of everyone around them in a negative way. Not you; nope, not anymore.

Although, this does not mean that you lose your empathy for people in pain because it is important to understand how someone else feels and find solutions to their particular ordeal. However, someone else's emotions should not consume yours in any way because it is not helpful to the person in need or you, if you fall into their state of being. They need an emotionally strong person to guide them, and you need to be strong to maintain your health and well-being.

Celebrate your positive emotion and reflect on the positive aspects of your life. It is easy to get caught up in the negative things that happen to us, but negative things should never contribute to a complete loss of emotion in any moment or day, and certainly not in our life as a whole. If you take the time to remember the good things in you life, it makes it easier to confront the bad things that occur. Positive emotions build resilience, provide fulfillment in work and personal relationships, help us confront adverse moments, and are a key to emotional intelligence.

You must also reflect on your negative feelings in order to connect with the reasons for their intrusion in your life. You become a well-round person emotionally when you are able to deal with the emotions that hurt you. As we have discussed, a person with high EQ confronts their negative emotions and does not push them away or ignore them.

Always question your own opinions. We are instinctively drawn to the viewpoints of people and outlets that support our opinion, and because of it, we become lost in our own ideology. Consequently, we become very rigid in our beliefs. Notions that might be healthy for your state of being may not be a comfortable place for everyone else. We do not have to agree with anyone, but we should not condemn people for their opinions, and we most certainly should not allow the opinions of someone else to influence us emotionally in a negative way. It is so easy to find opinions that match our own because there is so much information readily available, but it is crucial for people seeking emotional intelligence to take some to challenge their views by reading the perspective of people with opposing points of view. It is good practice in order to be receptive to new ideas.

Step outside of yourself and look at YOU objectively. You must understand yourself completely in order to master emotional intelligence. It is very difficult to look at yourself objectively, so you must take into consideration what other people say about you, especially if they say it all the time, and especially if you hear the same criticisms from multiple sources. Are they all wrong or you are you just too stubborn to believe that you make bad choices or have some faults that you could improve? Look for patterns in your behavior that lead to emotionally charged moments, and do not argue with the facts about yourself.

Remove yourself from social media. Engage face-to-face with people instead of relying on that cold screen that loses so much in nuance and context. You do not enhance your emotional intelligence in any way by creeping through social media pages and supplanting hastily constructed comment-bombs and meaningless remarks along the way. Nothing is gained from those pathetic interactions. Those internet gathering spots are hardly "social" at all. Meet friends outside of your phone, tablet, or computer. Go find them in the open air of a free society.

Keep an EQ journal in order to better understand yourself and your emotional triggers. Reflect on every day as you consider every emotion that you felt and how you dealt with the feelings that overcame you. A diary helps considerably with self-examination and self-awareness. Occasionally, look back over your journal entries to find patterns of emotionally bad behavior, and write about the ways you plan to resolve them.

EMOTIONAL INTELLIGENCE

It is critical to determine what motivates you on a daily basis. One of the major keys to emotional intelligence is keeping focus on a single direction, and that direction should align with HAPPINESS. Often, we do not follow through on our goals towards happiness because we lose motivation. It is important that you figure out what motivates you before you can even begin to understand how to complete any task. large or small. What are you attempting to accomplish and does it contribute to your happiness? Find the motivation to complete things you start in a satisfactory way, or do not start them at all.

Escape from the world. Slow down and take some time for yourself. Disconnect by reading, meditating, or hiking a trail. Breaks are important to maintaining our mental health and our emotional intelligence.

Self-aware individuals with emotional intelligence develop their ability to recognize their emotions while they are occurring. Recognizing emotions as they occur allows high EQ individuals to be flexible and adapt to every emotional situation instead of running with their pure feelings. You must always accept your emotions, but you do not have to be rigid with them, so process them in a rational way before you react to them.

Predict you future emotions. Consider every situation before you go into it, and try to predict how you will feel in the end. Practice naming and accepting the feelings, and maintain self-control as those named emotions come into being. Think about appropriate reactions to the emotions beforehand, so that it is easier to deal with them in a rational way once they arrive.

Learn to trust and fine-tine your intuition. If the path becomes unclear and your emotions are disturbed, trust your instincts. Your subconscious is your friend in ambiguous situations, and can help guide you to a rational outcome.

Do not get angry. Do not express anger or vent to anyone about something that cannot change or has little impact on accomplishing your goals. If you get the reputation as a complainer (see below), it is hard to shake. Use your emotional energy for something productive.

Quit complaining. If you complain then it implies that you are a victim, and you are choosing to remain a victim instead of productively constructing a solution to the issue. An emotionally intelligent person rarely feels as if someone has victimized them, outside of obvious reasons that involve a crime. Instead of complaining, the emotionally intelligent person immediately begins to look for ways to privately resolve the issue in a rational way in a reasonable amount of time. A resolution might require the minds of a few people other than yourself to solve the problem, but the meetings with these people involves problem-solving, and not complaining.

Do not dwell on the past. High EQ people learn from their mistakes and then send them to the vault. They do not dwell on them. Instead, they recall them when stepping into a similar situation with the hopes to improve from their mistake, but they do not constantly worry about them. Emotionally intelligent people relish the opportunity to correct their mistakes when given the opportunity, but they do not push the issue.

Find ways to snap out of your emotional crisis. There is an old saying that "motion" can dictate our "emotion". Therefore, use your physical body to shake off the emotion that is eating you up. Attend an aerobic exercise class or go for a walk and focus on the rhythm of your movements. The jolt provides you with power away from the routine that had you sinking in your feelings.

Stay on schedule. If you do not have a schedule, then create one, and stick to it. A schedule helps keep you on task, and puts you in the direction of your goals. Whenever you feel unfocused or edgy visit your schedule for the day, week, month, year, and get moving in the right direction. Making a commitment reduces procrastination and any reason to dwell on conflict.

As a part of your schedule, map out personal goals that provide motivation for the short term, and direction for the long haul. Do something every day that improves YOU, and improving you could be practicing EQ or taking a cruise to escape for a bit. There is a way to get closer to you goals everyday, so write them out along with ways to accomplish them. Be realistic when planning your goals and understand that they may need to change when life throws something unexpected at you.

Step outside of your comfort zone. As you progress to a higher EQ and become more confident in your emotional abilities, challenge yourself frequently with life-enriching new experiences. Build, build, build, and build your confidence by giving new opportunities a shot, and also knowing that the "trying" part is the most important element, not being good at the task from the beginning.

Show genuine interest in the people and the opportunities around you. We will discuss emotional contagion in detail later, but your enthusiasm for people and opportunities is infectious. Not only will it infect you, but everyone in your presence when you show that you care.

Trust people. Lose the cynicism and give people a chance. It is certainly beneficial to use intuition to feel out the sociopaths that make their way into our lives, but start every relationship with some trust, and you might be surprised to find that people will trust you in return, and trust is the basis of any healthy relationship.

Surround yourself with alls things positive. Avoid toxic people in your personal life when you can, and associate yourself with positive people, who inspire and motivate you in refreshing ways. Also, maintain a positive outlook and stay optimistic when things do not go according to your plan. Setbacks and "failures" should be looked upon as opportunities to improve and to problem-solve for better results in the future.

Ask for help when you need it, and help people in need. Helping people to reach their goals, and seeing them succeed, is beneficial to emotional health. On the other hand, do not be afraid to ask for help when it is crucial to your pursuit of a goal.

Show genuine empathy for people. Understand that everyone has different feelings, desires, stresses, and fears. In addition, not everyone is as strong, resilient, objective, or as smart as you. You can look down upon people who do not have the same competencies as you, or you can accept their deficiencies and hope they will accept yours because you have weaknesses, too. The other option is to choose to have low EQ for the entirety of your existence, because emotional intelligence does not exist without empathy. You must allow other people's experiences, large to trivial, to resonate within you. You do not know the experiences and background of every person until you ask them, and even if you do ask, their experiences might not be relative to your experiences, but you must attempt to connect with the people around you in order to respond to them in an emotionally rational way.

Be someone who is approachable. Keep your door open regardless of your position, and when someone walks through your door, drop what you are doing and listen to them, or set up a time for a discussion later, but never pretend to be listening while you click through your emails, or do some other task.

Listen to people with empathetic ears. Allow people to talk without interruption before you brush them off as weak or ignorant. Remove your cynicism and put away your personal worries for a few minutes, and truly absorb the things that people are telling you, and wear their emotions for a minute. Look clearly from their point of view, and try to understand just enough to offer something useful that might help them. Sometimes your acknowledgement is all they need. While it would be helpful to open up to them by using a personal anecdote, sometimes they just want to hear that you understand their situation, and offer confirmation that it is fine for them to feel the way they do.

Travel in order to see different points of view. Remove yourself from your bubble and go see how other people live in the world. Traveling broadens horizons of the mind.

Talk to strangers. It makes no sense to travel somewhere and not get to know the people who live and work there. Emotionally intelligent people are curious about others and the world as a whole. If you are not naturally curious, you might become that way when you start talking to people you do not know. Every person is a rare being with an interesting life, because it is different from yours. It is crucial that you remove yourself from the safety of your social circle and inspect other people's views on life in order to gain emotional intelligence.

Develop a skill. You admire someone, right? You know someone who has some social tool that is missing from your toolbox. You can develop that missing skill through careful observation and practice. You could even go to the person who has the skill and ask them to teach you how to develop it in yourself. They might have great advice to offer, something that was way outside of what you might have considered. It could be easier than you thought.

Network at open events. Everyone has a reason for attending professional or personal networking events, and usually they are quick to share their reasons, which might align with yours. Networking events proved an easy way to practice your social skills and emotional intelligence.

Adjust your body language accordingly. One thing that EQ experts seldom discuss, but is very important to emotional intelligence is what your body is telling people. You might have the best intentions while practicing your EQ verbally, but your body language could be expressing something completely different from what you want to come across to the people in your presence.

Posture is a huge component to emotional makeup, and your nonverbal communication must be on point with your verbal offerings. In addition, maintain eye contact and use a voice with the proper tone.

Do not be selfish. It is important that each of us looks out for our best interests, but complete and utter selfishness is not the motive to a balanced and emotionally intelligent person. Healthy people with solid EQ build up the people around them, help those people excel when they can, show appreciation for everyone's hard work, and are enthusiastic when other people succeed. The goal for the high EQ person is to rise up the chain of command, but no one has to go down for the emotionally intelligent person to succeed, and they also understand that nothing is done alone.

Do not be overly critical. Everyone needs a proper critique from time to time. Productive criticism helps us grow as individuals. However, harsh criticism with an acidic tone lowers morale and can crush someone's esteem and productive output. Some people are more sensitive than others, and emotionally intelligent people understand how to approach people of all personality types and how to use criticism for positive gain for everyone involved.

Do not give into negative peer pressure. Knowing what we do about emotionally intelligent people, it would almost be a disgrace if they were people who gave into peer pressure. People with a high EQ are independent forces of nature that would never succumb to the negative influences of the people around them or conform to please other people.

Eat as if you care about yourself. Eat a diet that is rich, balanced, and wholesome. If you are not eating, or you are eating too much, you must stop those bad habits, and put together a diet that nurtures your physical health and feeds your brain, so that you can tackle highly-charged situations with emotional intelligence.

Do not grow impatient with you progress because emotional intelligence requires a lifetime of dedication. High EQ takes practice and dedication to continual improvement. Revel in the process and every situation in which you own your emotions. Always figure out where your emotions were born, and make rational decisions. Even if that one good EQ moment in the day was sandwiched between two bad ones, it is still a victory worth recognizing.

EMOTIONAL INTELLIGENCE AND PERSONAL RELATIONSHIPS

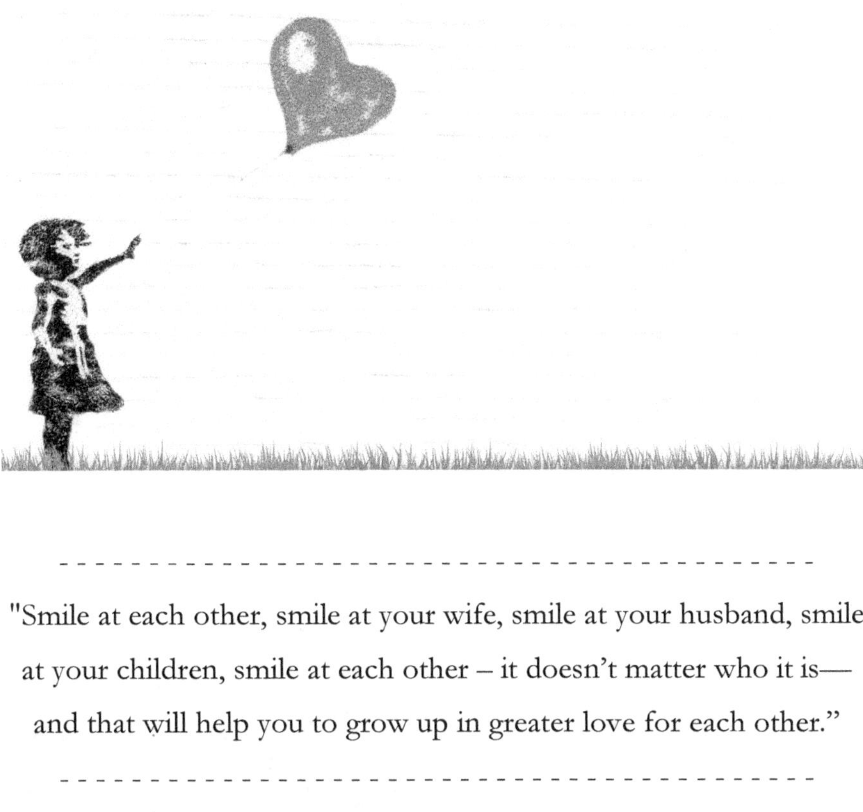

"Smile at each other, smile at your wife, smile at your husband, smile at your children, smile at each other – it doesn't matter who it is— and that will help you to grow up in greater love for each other."

Saint Teresa of Calcutta

Social interaction determines the success or failure of a personal relationship, and our emotions drive our social interactions whether they are with our partners, children, parents, siblings, or friends. While unconditional love drives relationships with family members, the same is not always true with friendships and romantic partnerships, which involve other factors that fall into the compatibility area.

Compatibility with a friend or partner involves life experiences, values, goals, interests, and you guessed it, emotional intelligence. Studies show that people with high EQ make better relationship partners.

If your relationship with your partner is a struggle, it is probably because one or both of you have a low EQ. There are ways to tell if your relationship needs to become emotionally intelligent.

The following are the most prominent signs that your relationship needs a lift in the EQ department:

- Obviously, if one of you cannot control their emotions then there is no need to look at the rest of the list. Emotionally intelligent people do not lash out at other people, and they do not get overly excited for no apparent reason.

EMOTIONAL INTELLIGENCE

- If you or your partner are clueless about the feelings of the other then the relationship lacks emotional intelligence. If you cannot read your partner's emotional cues of displeasure or your partner thinks your happiness is some sort of contempt, there will always be issues with connecting in an emotionally healthy way.

- Along the same lines as above, a person with a low EQ does not pick up on the tone of a conversation, and cannot accurately identify that someone is upset.

- On the other hand, you or your partner have low emotional intelligence if they cannot read you or you cannot be read because one of you maintains a poker face, pushes away emotions, and takes passive-aggressive attitudes instead of expressing feelings and working on issues.

- People with low EQ do not understand that they are saying something that is upsetting or hurtful, and they have bad timing when it comes to making jokes because they are socially immature or emotionally inappropriate.

- Do you or your partner have trouble maintaining friendships, and does one or both of you have trouble getting along with colleagues at work? These things indicate a low EQ, and it will eventually carry into the relationship.

- People with low EQ have limited or no empathy. Therefore, they do not know how to deal with people when they are feeling sorrow or other emotional pains. They might even trivialize emotions in general and downplay the need to show them. However, emotions are critical in a crisis, and relationships do experience critical points in which emotions must be expressed in a healthy way instead of avoided.

- If you or your partner are all over the place with internal emotions, or one of you is loud about every fluctuation from median emotions, then EQ dominates the relationship.

- Finally, if you or your partner does not feel touched by some emotion during movies, whether they are romantic of horrific, your relationship may have low EQ. In addition, if they do not "get" your dog, or you do not get theirs, and therefore, one of you does not appreciate the needs of the pup, then he, she, or you need some work in the EQ department.

Improving Your Relationship's Emotional Intelligence

If you have invested a lot in your relationship or there are other reasons why you wish to maintain it, there are ways for your partner to improve their EQ, if they are willing.

Alternatively, if you have a low EQ and want to improve your relationship, it is always possible, and with a little self-help, you can avoid the expense of a counselor.

It starts with positive criticism, laughing together at life's joys and wonders, sharing thoughts and feelings in a non-combative way, and support and encouragement of each other during trying times.

For a marriage or other romantic relationship to thrive, you and your partner have to be aware of each other's emotional needs, so that you both of you are capable of lifting up the other when life become chaotic. Be aware in the relationship, look for signs of trouble, and help your partner grow. If these things occur, your partner finds inspiration, and motivation for the long haul, as you chase individual and partnership goals and find happiness together.

If you need a fresh start towards those goals, and you and your partner are willing to work on emotional intelligence together, then do the following: You and your partner make lists independent of one another that include three emotional elements that you need in the relationship. Then, make another list of the three emotional elements that you think your partner needs. Finally, exchange lists, talk about the results, and brainstorm ways that both of you can do a better job of meeting each other's needs.

Emotional Contagion in Relationships

Anger and anxiety create difficult relationships, and depression has a long-lasting negative impact on a romantic partnership. It takes two very strong people and a lot of love to recover from some emotions and low EQ moments that bring about rage and unhealthy behavior that approaches or gets to self-destructive or abusive actions.

The goal in turning a relationship around and hitting a high-EQ stride is finding optimism in the smallest things, finding confidence in moments where there is a spark, being tenacious in your drive to make better emotional decisions with each new day, and showing enthusiasm when successes are reached through emotional intelligence practice routines. Be productive within the relationship, and do not ever get lazy.

Some relationships are not salvageable because too much emotional damage has been done by one person or the other. Another sad fact is that an emotionally *healthy* person can be in such a chaotic relationship with a person of exceedingly low emotional intelligence that they catch low EQ as if it is a virus. Psychologists even have a name for it: emotional contagion.

Emotional contagion is an infection of the emotional soul that can pass from one person to another, and it can literally wreck a person's life on all fronts from friendships to professional relationships.

On the other hand, confidence and enthusiasm can do the same thing, so it can all be turned around if you work hard at creating positive emotional outcomes and spreading them to your partner like a magic spell.

The first part involves taking your emotional vitamins, and in some cases, your emotional steroids, antibiotics, or antivirus, depending on the seriousness of your partner's condition, so that you do not catch the emotional virus. This involves your ability to relax on cue when your partner becomes emotionally disturbed.

Once you develop the ability to relax your emotions and avoid "two" angry, anxious, fearful, or frustrated people, you can begin to turn the emotions around to your favor by framing the situation in an objective way, so that you can maintain perspective.

When both members of the partnership are rigid with their emotions, it prevents solid interpretations of the situation, and behavior becomes counterproductive of any proper resolution. Both people raise their voices because *their* bad emotions are way more important to express loudly than the other person's conflicted emotions, or someone leaves the room, or even the house to avoid the confrontation completely.

When one partner, or both, practice high EQ, or have emotional intelligence, a shouting match does not occur, and one does not run away from the other. Instead, the relationship is guided to safety by proper emotional perspective. Unless you are dealing with a sociopath, which is a possibility, your emotionally intelligent behavior will be contagious, and the cliff will be avoided.

High or low emotional intelligence influences the person we fall in love with, and high or low EQ impacts how those relationships form over time. If the partnership has faltered because you or your significant other got emotionally lazy, and is showing decreased emotional EQ, it is time to tighten things up and take some continuing education courses for the emotional and mental health and well-being of the relationship, and each other.

A relationship with a low EQ has negative consequences in all areas of a person's life, including the professional realm, so practice, and get fixed, in order to save your relationship and improve your life as a whole.

THE OTHER SIDE OF EMOTIONAL INTELLIGENCE

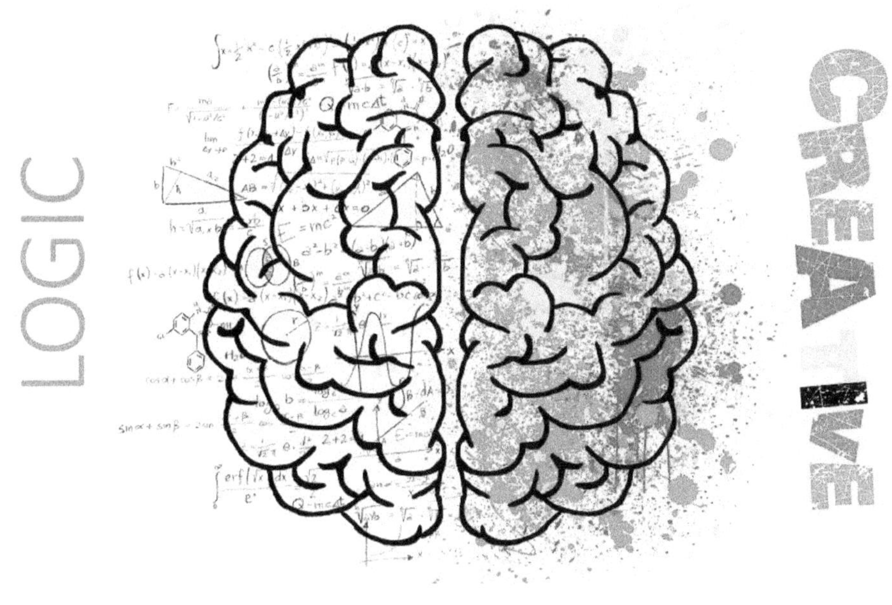

"Let's not forget that the little emotions are the great captains of our lives and we obey them without realizing it."

Vincent Van Gogh, Dutch painter

L et us be open. Nothing in life is as perfect as it might seem, and we can say the same for emotional intelligence.

Like anything else, once a person becomes more skilled at something, they can choose to use if for good or evil. Those who choose evil could hone their emotional intelligence skills and use them to manipulate people for their selfish desires.

Sociopaths are masters at emotional intelligence, and they are also manipulators who destroy people's lives. Therefore, in the wrong hands, high EQ could have horrible consequences on individual people.

When you can control your emotions, or create emotions from thin air, you can disguise the true nature of your feelings. When you have the ability to tune into the emotions of other people, you can improvise empathy and influence people to follow you wherever you might lead them.

Social scientists understand this impact. When a leader gives an emotional speech that implies empathy and provides inspiration, the audience members remember very little of the message because they lose the motivation to scrutinize the message, though they claim to recall it, while simultaneously feeling kinship with the speaker.

EMOTIONAL INTELLIGENCE

This is called the "awe struck" effect, and it used for good and evil. The good can be found in many of Martin Luther King's speeches in which he promotes civil disobedience for the cause of civil liberties. We study those speeches today because of the impact they had on large group of people, and because those speeches got many people to move in one direction.

Who does not feel some sort of emotion when they hear King's "I have a dream" speech? It tugs at our very soul to deliver on his vision that "on the red hills of Georgia sons of former slaves and the sons of former slave-owners will be able to sit down together at the table of brotherhood."

The speech was perfect in its rich balance of rational reasoning and hearty emotion. People who supported his emotional appeal, which King brought to his audiences with emotional intelligence, fought hard for the justice of all Americans. On the other hand, people with low EQ found his ideals disturbing, and formed plans to kill King, and someone finally did.

Keep in mind, Hitler had the same responses from the audiences who heard his "inspiring" speeches of hate and doom. The response to his speeches was devastating in its results, as millions of people died during a systematic genocide.

Leaders with Machiavellian qualities use emotional intelligence as a weapon to get to higher ground, and they do it in the worst ways. In another one of my books, I explain the Machiavellian in detail. The following is a piece from the book.

According to the Florence philosopher Machiavelli, who lived in the late 15h Century and the early 16th century, honesty and moral virtue are something to toss aside if people in leadership positions can gain more power and control through treachery and deceit. In fact, Machiavelli said that anyone who wishes to rise upward should manipulate their followers even if it does not come natural to them.

In modern psychology, the term "Machiavellian" does not include those people with a conscience who occasionally turn down its volume in order to gain more power. Instead, psychologists reserve the term for people with a personality disorder whose minds willfully power them to become master manipulators.

Plain and simple, these villains of society are amoral to their core. They are calculating, crooked, and cleverly conniving. Everyone around the Machiavellian is a disposable stepping-stone to get to the next level. They are amoral and immoral in a conventional sense because they are only concerned with getting a result, and they do not care how they obtain it.

EMOTIONAL INTELLIGENCE

Machiavellians control their impulses and are patient opportunists through a combination of cynicism and emotional detachment. They use superficial charm, self-disclosure, guilt, and pressure as manipulative tactics. While they might stoop to threats and force when it is necessary to get what they need, they prefer to use subtle tactics in order to assure plausible deniability. They do not make long-term ideological commitments because short-term achievement is their driving force.

When you see these characteristics in someone, it is crucial that you do not shake it off or allow them to penetrate your life in a substantial way. They do not make good friends, spouses, or colleagues because they make up part of the "Dark Triad," which also includes psychopaths and narcissists.

A research team at the University College London is on a mission to shine the light on the dark side of high EQ. Their contention is that emotionally intelligent people "intentionally shape their emotions to fabricate favorable impressions of themselves" by disguising their real emotions and true intentions.

The leader of the research team, Martin Kilduff, does not mince words when describing his contention, writing, "The strategic disguise of one's emotions and the manipulation of others' emotions for strategic ends are behaviors evident not only on Shakespeare's stage but also in the offices and corridors where power and influence are traded."

Even those who would never call themselves devious use emotional intelligence to manipulate. They include nearly all the successful people we discussed in the first few chapters. They use EQ as a means to accomplish goals, but they are not trying to hurt anyone.

For example, in a journal article titled *An Alternative to Bureaucratic Impersonality and Emotional Labor*, which sounds to me like a fancy way of saying "emotional intelligence", a Stanford research team studied a company called the Body Shop. They found that the founder of the company used high EQ to manipulate her staff, and she even admitted it.

"Whenever we wanted to persuade our staff to support a particular project," founder Anita Roddick confided, "we always tried to break their hearts."

Manipulation and motivation is a fine line. The point here is that we cannot assume that people are studying and implementing emotional intelligence for good and selfless reasons, instead of for nefarious reasons. We have to be careful when using it, and also recognize when it is being used against us with evil intention.

CONCLUSION

"There's only one corner of the universe you can be certain of improving, and that's your own self."

Aldous Huxley, English writer

Psychologist Adam Grant did a study and wrote a paper on emotional intelligence called *Rocking the Boat but Keeping it Steady: The Role of Emotion in Employee Voice* for the Academy of Management. Yes, this is the same professor hat debated Dan Goleman over the importance of EQ in the workplace, and even called it overrated

The professor at the University of Pennsylvania was attempting to solve the riddle of high EQ. He wondered how employees with emotional intelligence might challenge the status quo. In his research at a healthcare company, he found out that high EQ staff members spoke up more often and with more effect.

When they felt that their peers were being treated unfairly, they made it clear that they did not improve of the treatment. However, these high-EQ individuals reacted without anger and used reason to explain the injustice. In addition, they brought innovative ideas to senior leaders without fear of rejection and with an expression of contagious enthusiasm.

Even Grant, an EQ skeptic, found positive results when studying emotional intelligence. Emotional intelligence is the real deal. It has been proven impactful for decades, and philosophized for centuries, as a prudent way to get ahead of your competition as you ascend to leadership positions. In addition, it improves your mental health and emotional stability, and your personal relationships.

Keep practicing. Emotions should always work FOR YOU, not against you. There is no need to counterattack every attack against you, or declare yourself a victim of someone else's horrible scheme against you.

You must own your emotions and use them for the good of your own health and personal successes. Do not be troubled by the low EQ of the people around you. Rise above it all on wave of emotional intelligence.

www.ingramcontent.com/pod-product-compliance
Lightning Source LLC
Chambersburg PA
CBHW060750260726
48660CB00002B/562